PHIL COLLINS

GOLD

Published by:
Wise Publications,
14-15 Berners Street, London W1T 3LJ, UK.

Exclusive Distributors:
Music Sales Limited,
Distribution Centre, Newmarket Road, Bury St Edmunds, Suffolk IP33 3YB, UK.
Music Sales Pty Limited,
20 Resolution Drive, Caringbah, NSW 2229, Australia.

Order No. AM1002760
ISBN 978-1-84938-964-8
This book © Copyright 2011 by Wise Publications,
a division of Music Sales Limited..

Edited by Jenni Wheeler.

Printed in the EU.

Your Guarantee of Quality

As publishers, we strive to produce every book
to the highest commercial standards.

This book has been carefully designed to minimise awkward
page turns and to make playing from it a real pleasure.

Particular care has been given to specifying acid-free, neutral-sized
paper made from pulps which have not been elemental chlorine bleached.
This pulp is from farmed sustainable forests and was produced
with special regard for the environment.

Throughout, the printing and binding have been planned to ensure
a sturdy, attractive publication which should give years of enjoyment.
If your copy fails to meet our high standards, please inform us
and we will gladly replace it.

www.musicsales.com

PHIL COLLINS

GOLD

WISE PUBLICATIONS
part of The Music Sales Group

London / New York / Paris / Sydney / Copenhagen / Berlin / Madrid / Hong Kong / Tokyo

Against All Odds
(Take A Look At Me Now)

Words & Music by Phil Collins

1. How can I just let you walk a-way, just let you leave with-out a trace? When I stand here tak-ing ev-'ry breath with you. Ooh, you're the

on - ly one who real - ly knew me___ at all.___

2. How can you just walk___ a - way from me when all I can do is watch you leave?___ 'Cause we've
(3.) wish I could just make___ you turn a - round, turn a - round and see me cry.___ There's so

shared the laugh - ter and___ the pain___ and e - ven shared___ the tears.___ You're the
much I need___ to say___ to you,___ so man - y rea - sons why.___

7

Another Day In Paradise

Words & Music by Phil Collins

1. She calls out__ to the man__ on the street,__ "Sir__ can you help__
(Verses 2, 3 & 4 (%) see block lyric)

__ me?" "It's cold__ and I've no - where to sleep,__

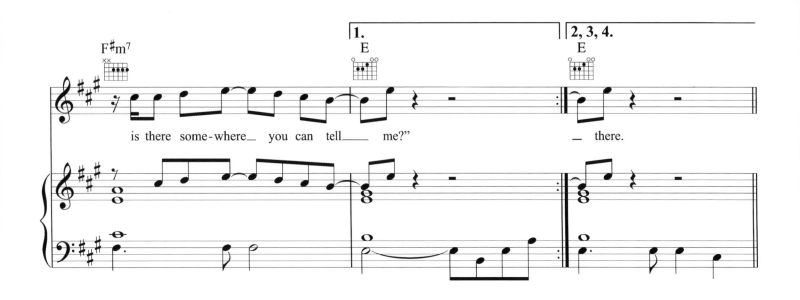

is there some-where__ you can tell__ me?"   __ there.

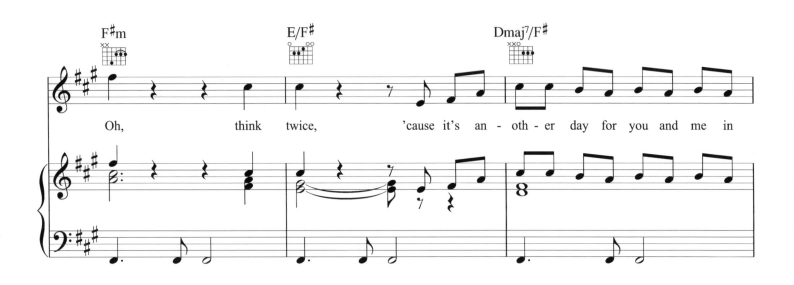

Oh,   think twice,   'cause it's an - oth - er day for you and me in

pa - ra - dise.__   Oh,   think twice,   'cause it's an -

-oth - er day for you,___ you and me in pa - ra - dise.___

(𝄋) Just think a - bout___ it Think a - bout_

___ it (𝄋) Think a - bout___ it

To Coda ⊕

13

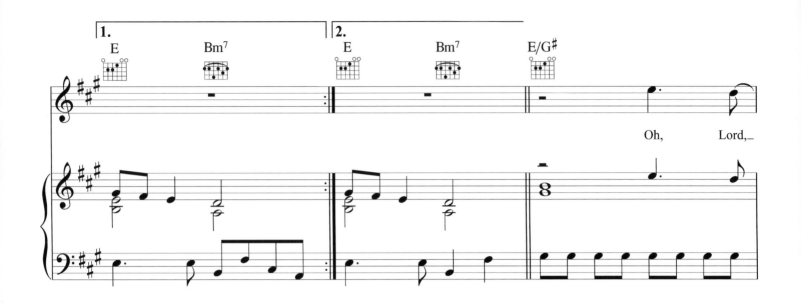

Oh, Lord,

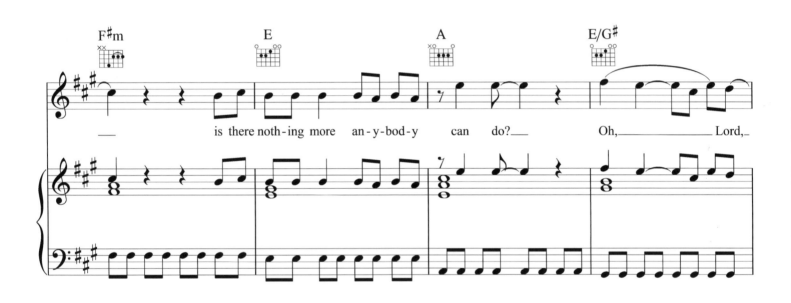

is there noth-ing more an-y-bod-y can do? Oh, Lord,

there must be some-thing you can say.

Verse 2:
He walks on, doesn't look back,
He pretends he can't hear her.
Starts to whistle as he crosses the street,
Seems embarrassed to be there.

Verse 3:
She calls out to the man on the street,
He can see she's been crying.
She's got blisters on the soles of her feet,
She can't walk but she's trying.

Verse 4: (𝄋)
You can tell from the lines on her face,
You can see that she's been there.
Probably been moved on from every place,
'Cause she didn't fit in there.

Easy Lover

Words by Phil Collins
Music by Phil Collins, Nathan East & Philip Bailey

try'n' to make____ you see.____ She's the kind of girl you dream____ of,
You're the one that wants to hold____ her,

dream____ of keep-ing hold of. Bet-ter for - get____
hold____ her and con - trol her. Bet-ter for - get____

____ it. You'll____ nev - er get it.____
____ it. You'll____ nev - er get it.____

She will play____ a - round and leave you,
'Cause she'll say____ that there's no oth - er

21

Follow You, Follow Me

Words & Music by Phil Collins, Tony Banks
& Mike Rutherford

23

pass - ing year there___ will be.___

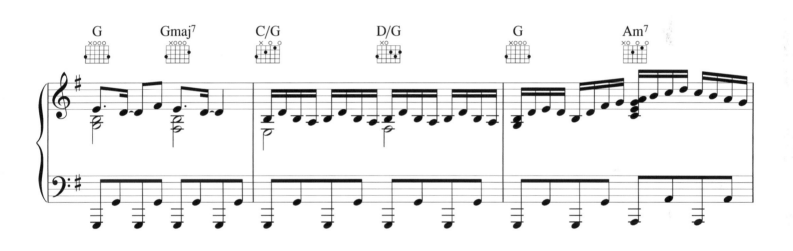

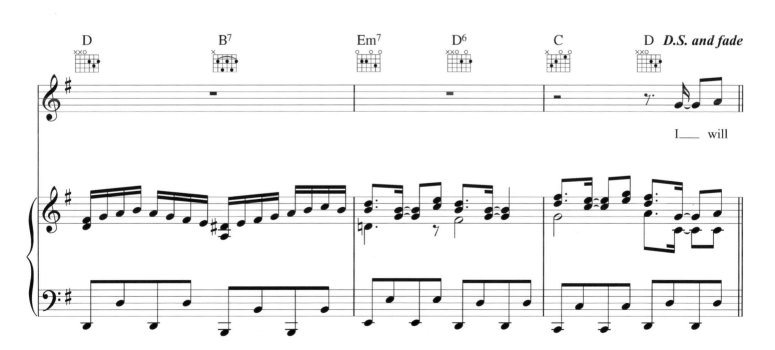

I___ will

Hold On My Heart

Words & Music by Phil Collins, Tony Banks
& Mike Rutherford

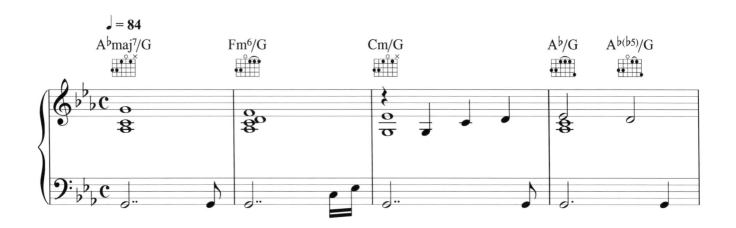

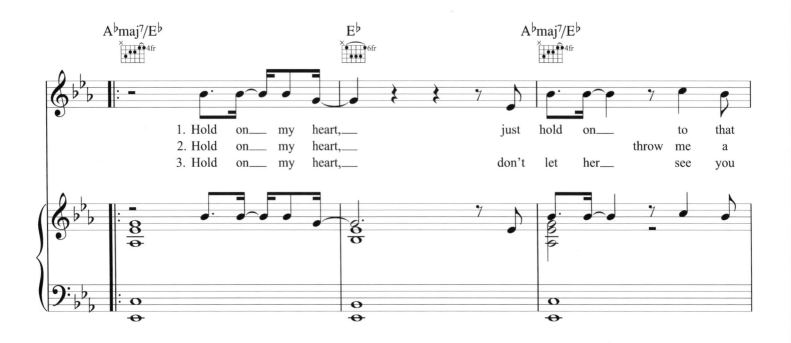

1. Hold   on___   my   heart,___   just   hold   on___   to   that
2. Hold   on___   my   heart,___   throw   me   a
3. Hold   on___   my   heart,___   don't   let   her___   see   you

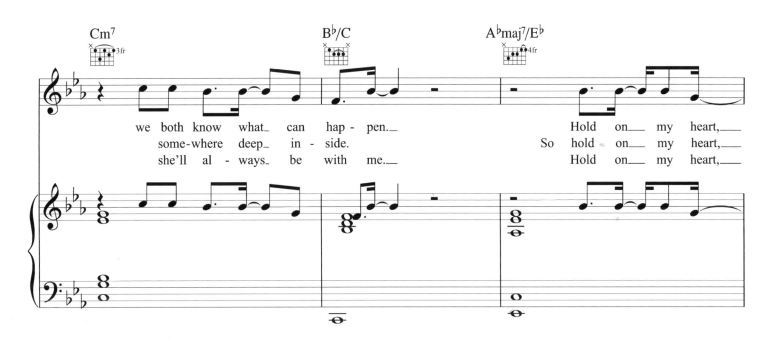

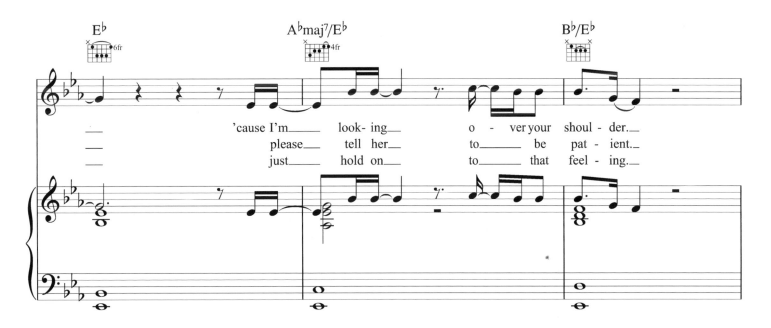

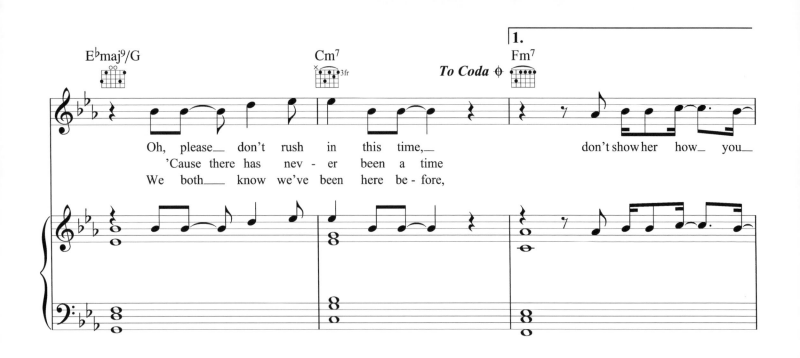

Oh, please___ don't rush in this time,___ don't show her how___ you
'Cause there has nev - er been a time
We both___ know we've been here be - fore,

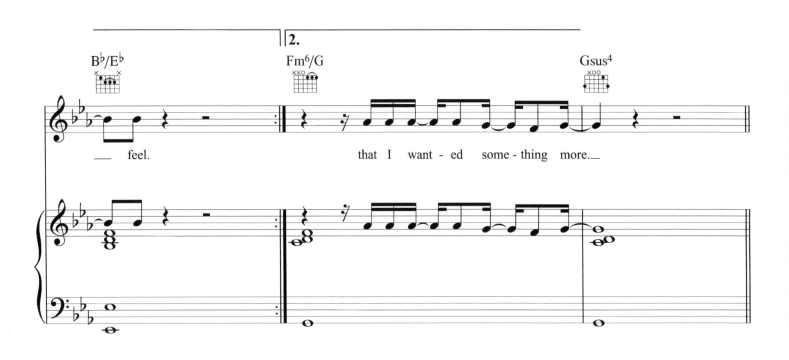

___ feel. that I want - ed some - thing more.___

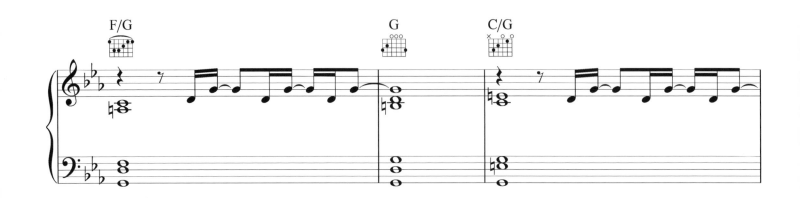

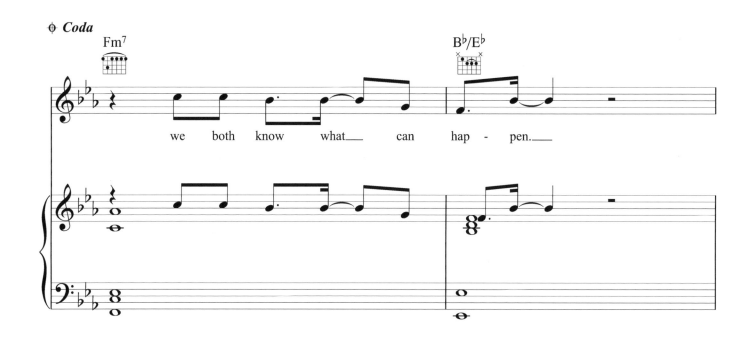

we both know what__ can hap - pen.__

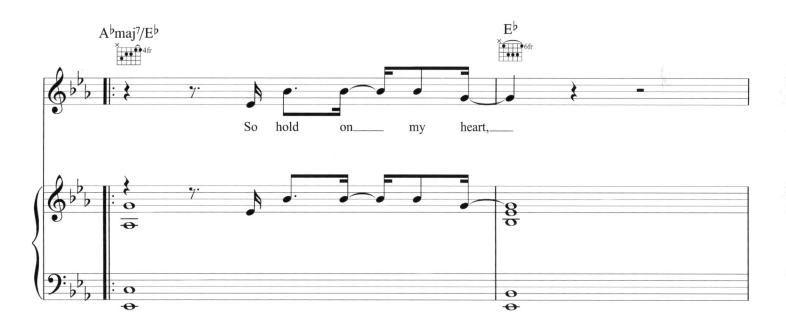

So hold on__ my heart,__

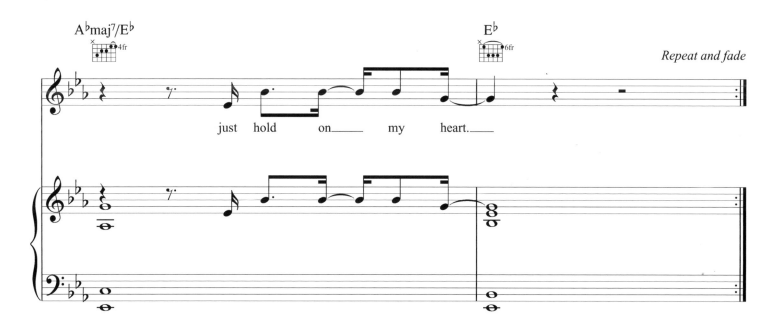

Repeat and fade

just hold on__ my heart.__

I Wish It Would Rain Down

Words & Music by Phil Collins

1. You know I nev - er meant to see you a - gain, and I
2. You said you did - n't need me in your life,
3. 'Cause I know, I know, I nev - er meant to 'cause you

on - ly passed by as a friend.____
oh, I guess you were right.____
no pain, and I re-al-ise I let you down.

All this time I stayed out of sight,____
Ooh, I nev-er meant to cause you no pain,____
But I know in my heart of hearts, I know I'm

I start-ed won-der-ing, why?____
but it looks like I did it a-gain.____
nev-er gon-na hurt you a-gain.____

Now I,

In The Air Tonight

Words & Music by Phil Collins

39

wipe off that grin, I know where you've been, it's
hurt does-n't show but the pain still grows, it's no

all been a pack of lies.
stran-ger to you or me.

D.S. al Coda

Coda

I can feel it in the air to-night, oh Lord,

oh Lord.

41

If Leaving Me Is Easy

Words & Music by Phil Collins

hard - er.	Oh,	if leav-ing me	is eas- y,	then you

know	that com-ing back	is hard-er,	woo.	*(sax solo)*

Fade out

Invisible Touch

Words & Music by Phil Collins, Tony Banks
& Mike Rutherford

Moderately, with a strong backbeat

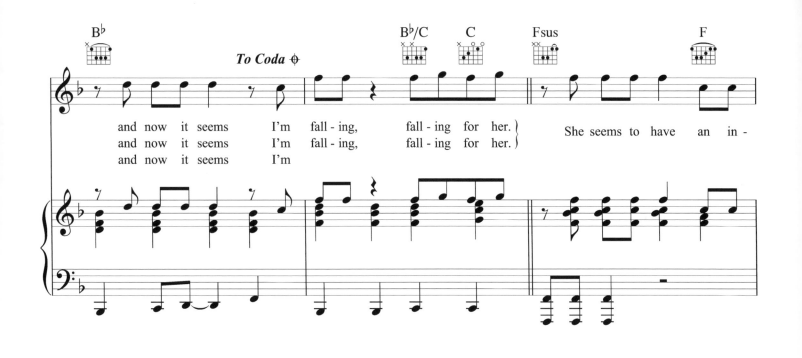

and now it seems I'm fall - ing, fall - ing for her. She seems to have an in -
and now it seems I'm fall - ing, fall - ing for her.
and now it seems I'm

-vis - i - ble touch, yeah, she reach-es in___ and grabs right hold of your heart.

She seems to have an in - vis - i - ble touch, yeah, it takes con - trol___ and

slow - ly tears___ you a - part.

She seems to have an in - vis - i - ble touch, yeah,
She seems to have an in - vis - i - ble touch, yeah,

she reach - es in___ and grabs right hold of your heart.
it takes con - trol___ and

1. slow - ly tears___ you a - part.
2. *D.S. al Coda*

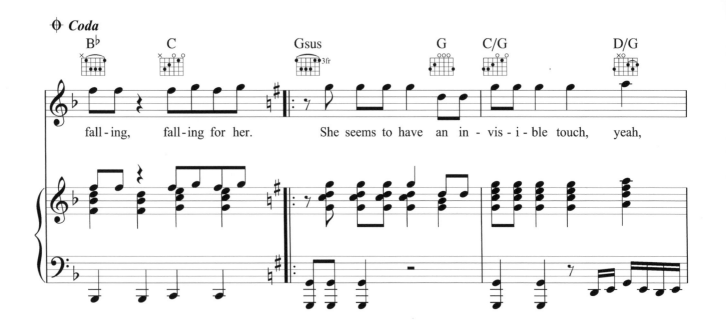

No Son Of Mine

Words & Music by Phil Collins, Tony Banks
& Mike Rutherford

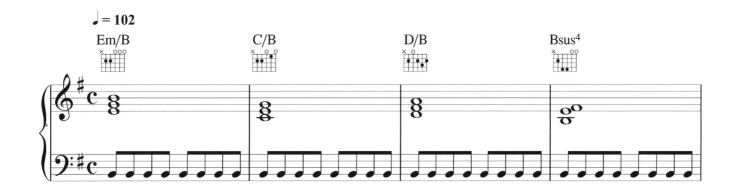

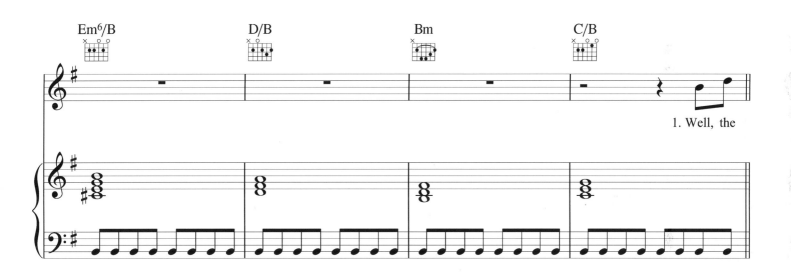

1. Well, the

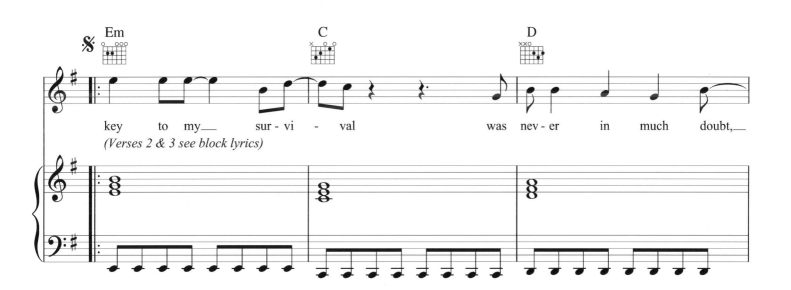

key to my___ sur-vi -val was nev-er in much doubt,___
(Verses 2 & 3 see block lyrics)

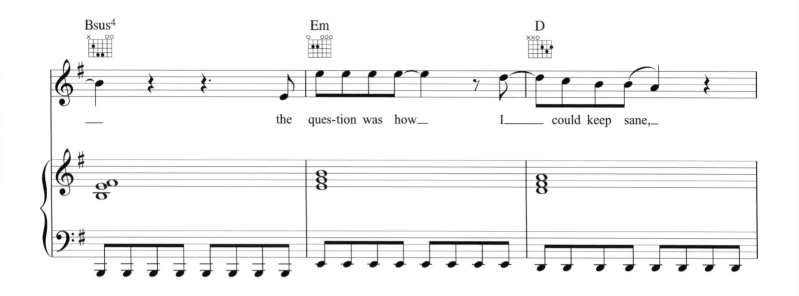

the ques-tion was how__ I_____ could keep sane,_

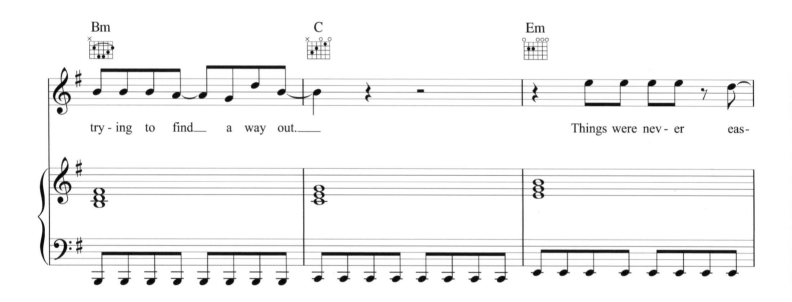

try - ing to find__ a way out.___ Things were nev - er eas-

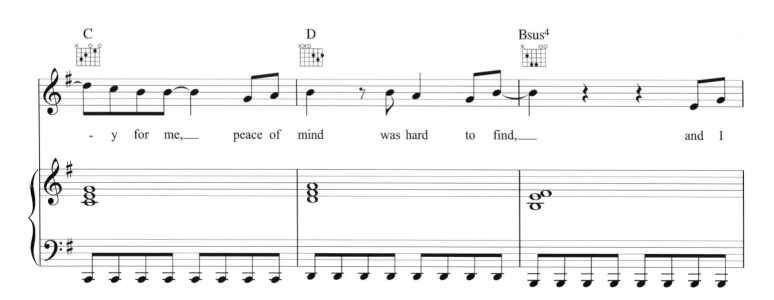

- y for me,__ peace of mind was hard to find,___ and I

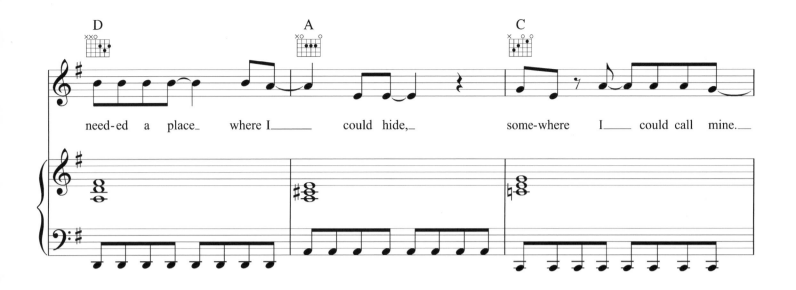

need-ed a place_ where I_____ could hide,_____ some-where I_____ could call mine.____

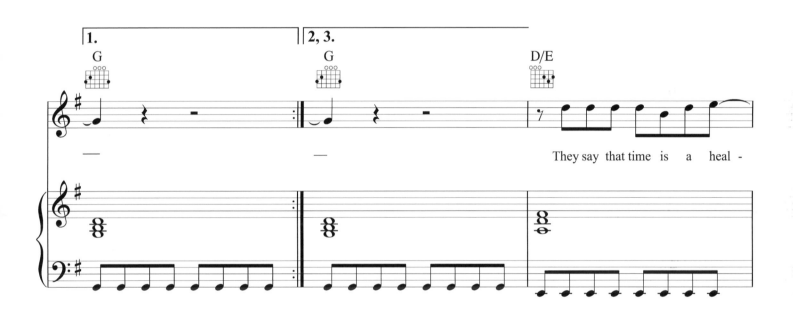

1. **2, 3.**

_____ ― ― They say that time is a heal -

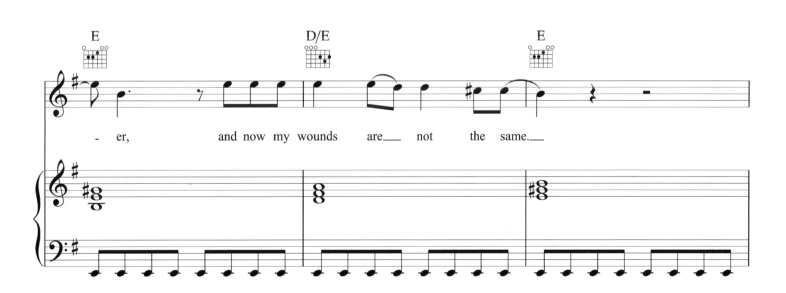

-er, and now my wounds are_____ not the same.____

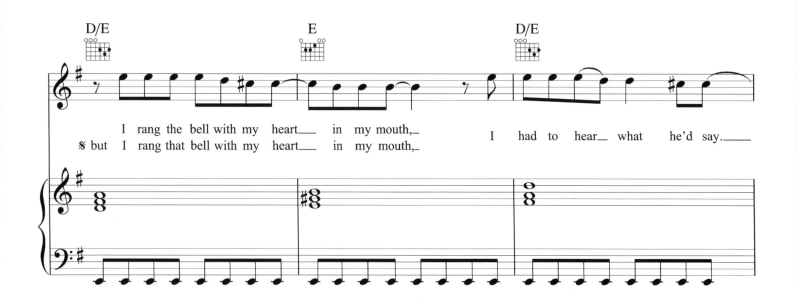

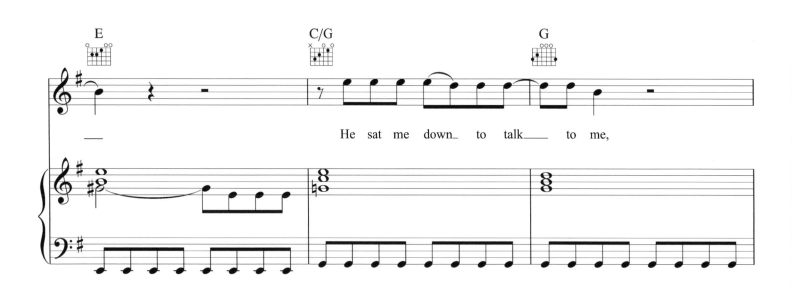

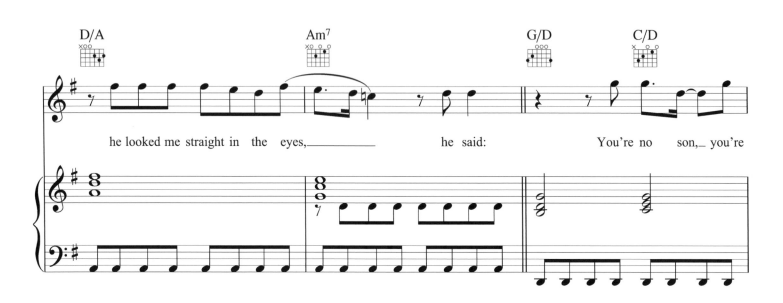

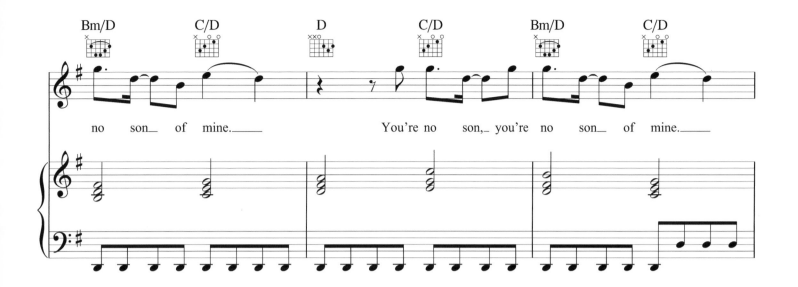

no son of mine._____ You're no son,_ you're no son of mine._____

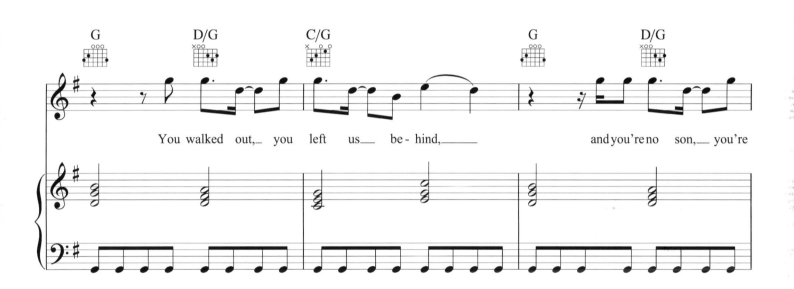

You walked out,_ you left us__ be-hind,_____ and you're no son,_ you're

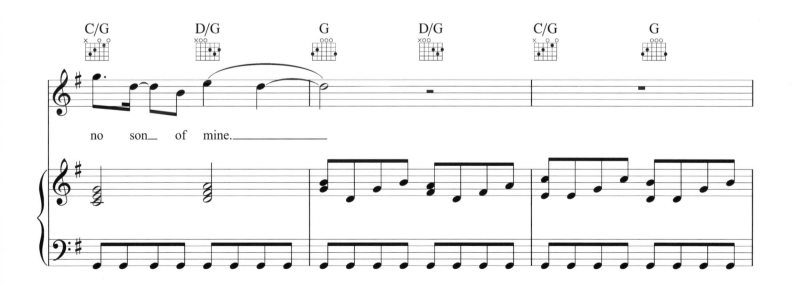

no son_ of mine._____

Oh, his words how_ they hurt me, I'll nev - er for - get it,

and as the time it__ went by,__ I lived to re - gret

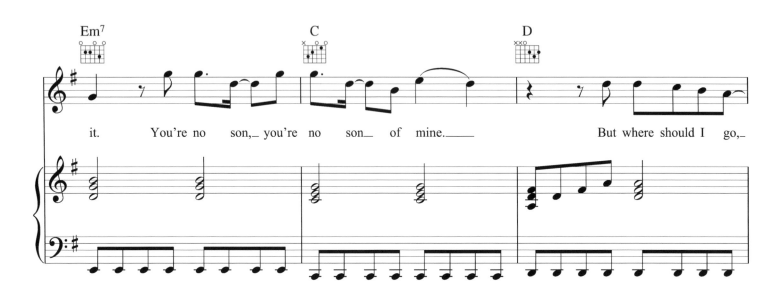

it. You're no son,_ you're no son_ of mine.____ But where should I go,_

and what should I do?___ You're no son,_ you're no son_ of mine._____

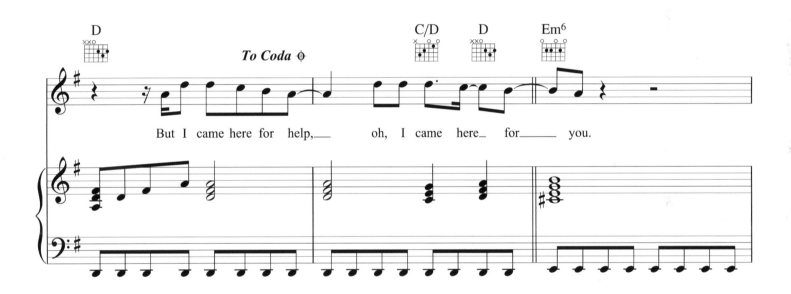

But I came here for help,___ oh, I came here_ for_____ you.

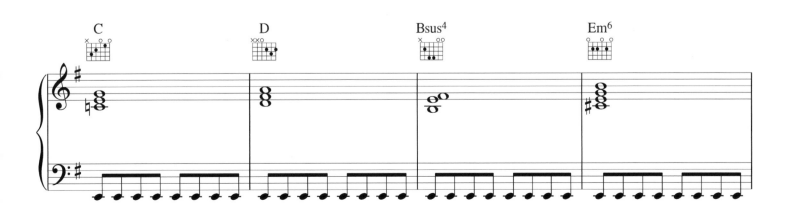

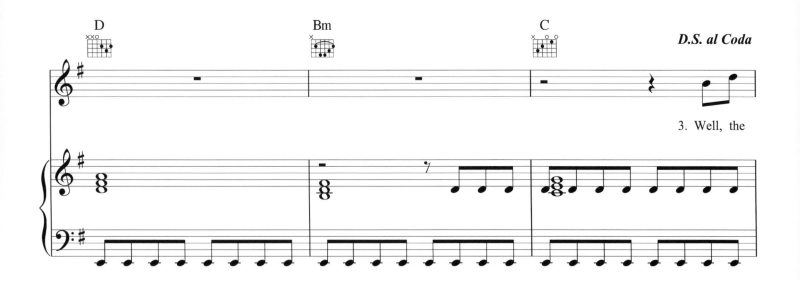

D.S. al Coda

3. Well, the

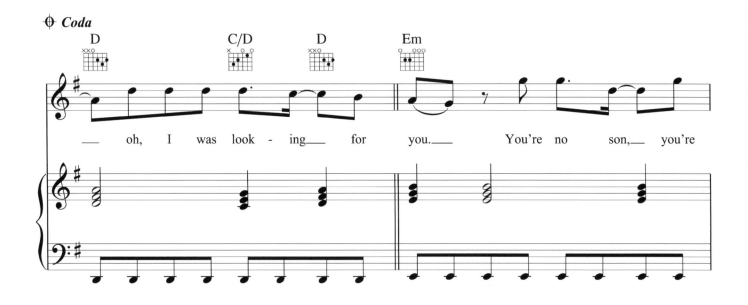

Coda

— oh, I was look - ing— for you.— You're no son,— you're

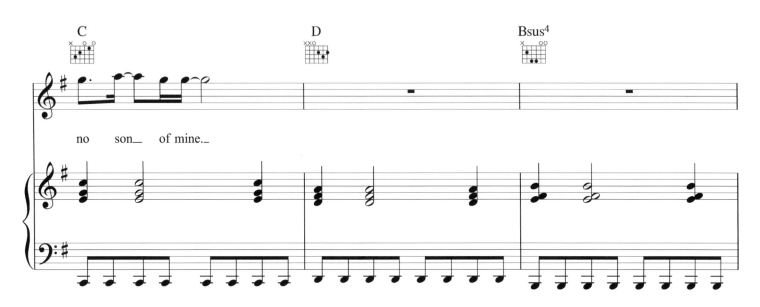

no son— of mine.—

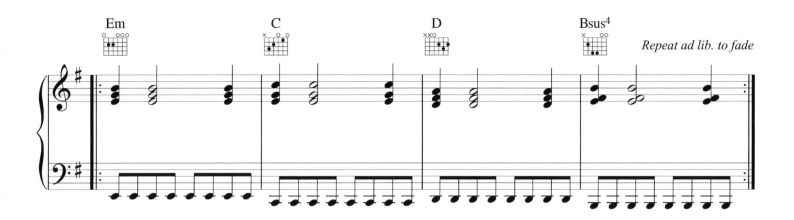

Verse 2

I didn't think much about it
Till it started happening all the time.
Soon I was living with the fear everyday
Of what might happen that night.
I couldn't stand to hear the crying
Of my mother, and I remember when
I swore that that would be the last they'd see of me,
And I never went home again.

Verse 3

Well, the years passed so slowly,
I thought about him every day,
What would I do if we passed on the street,
Would I keep running away?
In and out of hiding places,
Soon I'd have to face the facts,
That we'd have to sit down and talk it over,
And that would mean going back.

That's All

Words & Music by Phil Collins, Tony Banks
& Mike Rutherford

Just as I thought____ it was go-ing al-right, I found out I'm wrong____ when I thought I was right. It's al-ways the same,____ it's just a shame, that's all.____

till   the end.

C   D   Em   Am⁷   D

Am⁷   D   Am⁷   D   Em

D.S. al Coda

Well, I could

𝄶 *Coda*

Em

till   the end.   But just as I   thought_ it was go-ing al-right,   I found out I'm wrong_

67

One More Night

Words & Music by Phil Collins

one____ more night,____ give me just one more night,__

just one more night____ 'cause I_____

____ can't wait____ for-ev- er.____ Like a riv-

-er to____ the sea,____ I will al - ways be____ with____

Turn It On Again

Words & Music by Phil Collins, Tony Banks
& Mike Rutherford

luck a - gain.
-oth - er day,

Down_ on my luck a - gain.
and__ we will fly a - way?

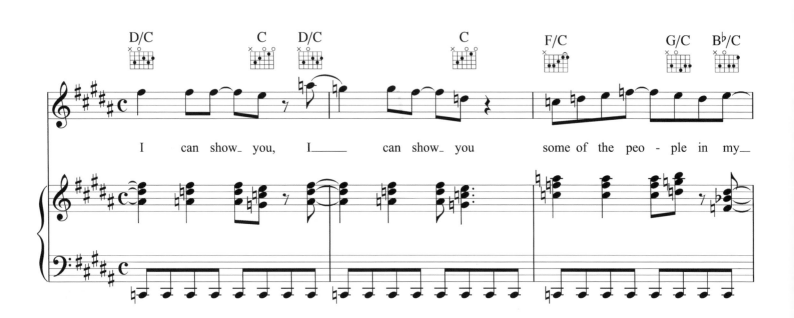

I can show_ you, I__ can show_ you some of the peo - ple in my_

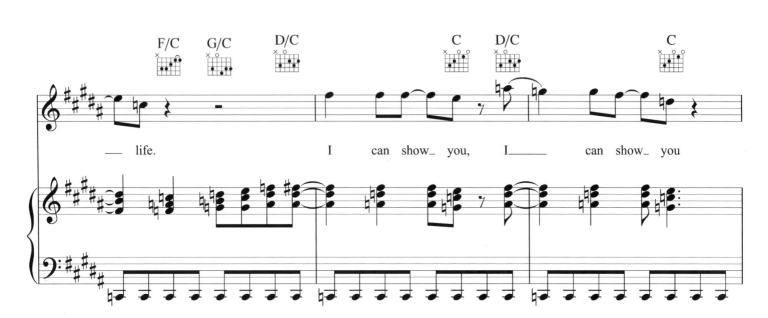

__ life. I can show_ you, I__ can show_ you

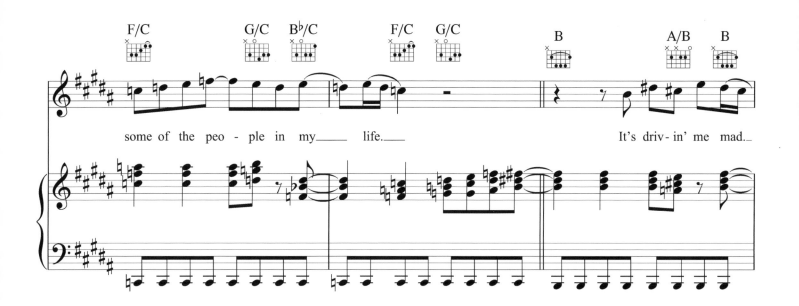

some of the peo - ple in my____ life.____ It's driv- in' me mad..

Just an - oth - er way of pass-ing the day.____

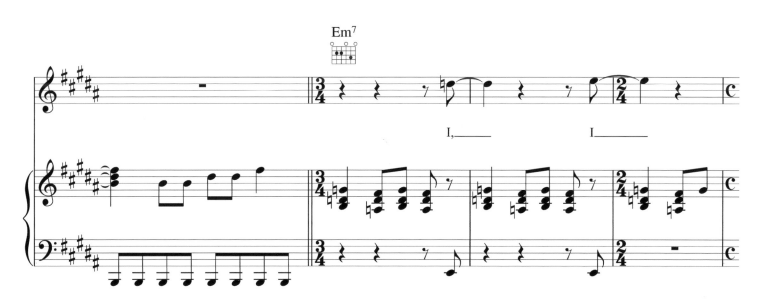

I,____ I____

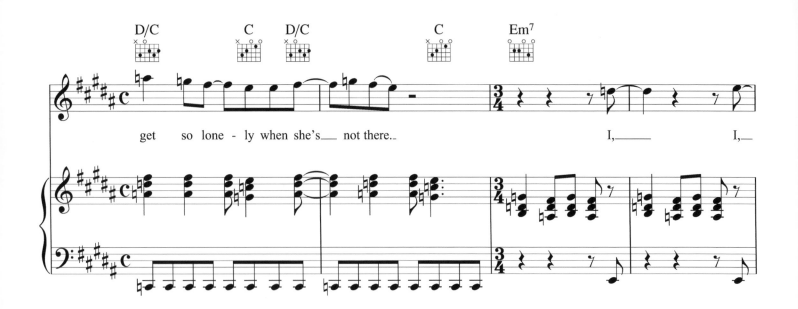

get so lone - ly when she's___ not there..

I,___ I,___

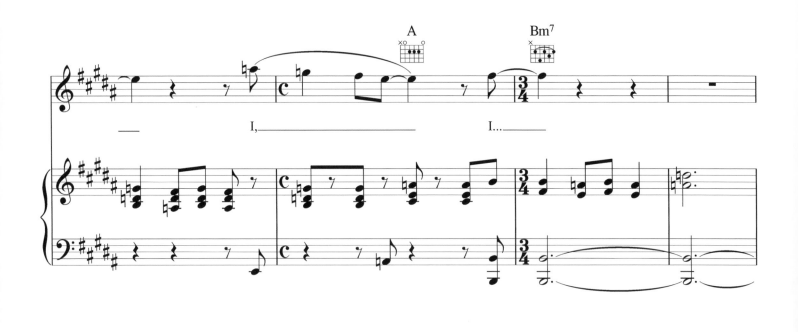

I,_____ I..._____

You're just___ an - oth - er face___

that I___ know from the   T. V. show.   I have known you for so

ver - y long.   I feel___   you   like   a friend.

D.S. al Coda

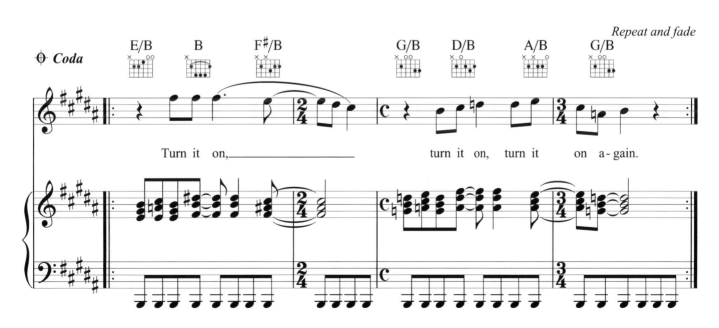

Turn it on,_____   turn it on, turn it   on a- gain.

Repeat and fade

You'll Be In My Heart

Words & Music by Phil Collins